Positive Affirmations

for

Black Teen Girls

This Book Belongs To

_____

_____

Introduction

Welcome to a journey of self-discovery, empowerment, and boundless potential. This book is dedicated to you, a black teen girl, brimming with unique qualities, dreams, and aspirations. Each page is filled with affirmations crafted to uplift, inspire, and remind you of your inherent worth and limitless capabilities.

In a world that often tries to define who you are, it's essential to cultivate a strong sense of self and embrace your individuality. You are more than enough, and this book is here to help you recognize and celebrate your true power. The affirmations within these pages are designed to support you through the various aspects of your life, encouraging you to love yourself unconditionally, believe in your abilities, and pursue your dreams with confidence and determination.

The themes explored in this book range from self-love and confidence to academic success and leadership, each chosen to address the diverse areas of your life where you can shine. Whether you are facing challenges, seeking motivation, or simply need a reminder of your brilliance, these affirmations will serve as your guide.

As you read and internalize these positive messages, remember that you are not alone. Countless other young women are on this journey with you, each finding strength and empowerment through their unique experiences. Embrace your path, celebrate your progress, and always know that you are a powerful force capable of achieving greatness.

This book is your companion, a source of encouragement, and a reminder of your extraordinary potential. Let these affirmations resonate with you, uplift you, and inspire you to be the best version of yourself. Your journey is unique, and your light is needed in this world.

With love,

Aaliyah Jones

Self-Love

I am beautiful, inside and out.

My worth is not defined by others' opinions.

I love and accept myself unconditionally.

I am deserving of all the love and kindness I

give to others.

I am proud of who I am becoming.

I am confident in my unique beauty.

I am enough just as I am.

I radiate self-love and inner peace.

My self-worth is immeasurable.

I honor and respect my body.

I deserve to take up space in this world.

My flaws make me perfect.

I am strong and resilient.

I embrace my individuality.

I am proud of my heritage and culture.

I deserve to be loved and cherished.

My happiness begins with me.

I choose to love myself more every day.

I am my own best friend.

I am a masterpiece in progress.

Notes

Magic

be the
·BEST·
version
of ★ you

LOVE
YOUR
SELF

Confidence

I believe in myself and my abilities.

I can achieve anything I set my mind to.

I am confident in my decisions.

My voice matters, and I will use it.

I am capable of achieving greatness.

I trust myself and my intuition.

I am confident in my unique talents.

I am not afraid to take risks.

I am proud of my accomplishments.

I am bold and courageous.

I can handle any challenge that comes my way.

I am worthy of my dreams and goals.

I believe in my potential to succeed.

I am unstoppable when I set my mind to something.

I am proud of who I am.

I am fearless and unapologetic.

I am confident in my ability to create change.

I am deserving of success and happiness.

I am my own biggest cheerleader.

I am powerful beyond measure.

Notes

Beautiful

Keep
GROWING

you
are
Awesome

JUST
Believe
IN
YOURSELF

Be
you

Strength

I am stronger than any challenge.

My strength comes from within.

I can overcome any obstacle.

I am resilient and capable.

I grow stronger every day.

I have the power to create my own path.

My strength inspires others.

I am a warrior in my own life.

I embrace my inner strength.

I am powerful and determined.

I can face any adversity with courage.

I am a beacon of strength and hope.

I am proud of my inner strength.

My strength lies in my compassion.

I am a survivor and a thriver.

I have the power to persevere.

I am not defined by my struggles.

I find strength in my vulnerability.

I am empowered by my challenges.

My strength is my superpower.

Notes

GIRL POWER

YOU GROW GIRL

amazing

Resilience

I am resilient and unbreakable.

I bounce back stronger from every setback.

I rise above all challenges.

My resilience knows no bounds.

I turn my pain into power.

I am a testament to resilience.

I thrive in the face of adversity.

I am resilient in mind, body, and spirit.

I turn obstacles into opportunities.

I am resilient in my pursuit of happiness.

I am unshakable in my determination.

I grow stronger with each challenge.

I am adaptable and resilient.

I find strength in my resilience.

I am a living example of perseverance.

My resilience shines through in tough times.

I face life's challenges with grace and strength.

I am a survivor.

I am empowered by my resilience.

My resilience is my greatest asset.

Notes

Academic Success

I am intelligent and capable.

I excel in my studies.

I am dedicated to my education.

I am focused and determined to succeed.

I am a lifelong learner.

I am proud of my academic achievements.

I am capable of mastering any subject.

I believe in my academic potential.

I am a successful student.

I am committed to my education.

I am an avid learner and a critical thinker.

I am proud of my intellectual abilities.

I embrace challenges as opportunities to learn.

I am capable of achieving academic greatness.

I am disciplined and motivated.

I am a diligent and hardworking student.

I am confident in my ability to learn and grow.

I am a successful and accomplished student.

I am worthy of academic success.

I am proud of my academic journey.

Notes

Friendships

I attract positive and supportive friends.

I am a loyal and caring friend.

I deserve meaningful and healthy friendships.

I am surrounded by people who uplift me.

I bring joy and positivity to my friendships.

I am valued and appreciated by my friends.

I am a good listener and a supportive friend.

I am grateful for my friendships.

I build strong and lasting connections.

I am kind and compassionate to my friends.

I am worthy of loyal and loving friends.

I nurture my friendships with love and care.

I am a source of positivity and encouragement.

I attract friends who inspire and motivate me.

I am a trustworthy and dependable friend.

I am grateful for the love and support of my

friends.

I am a friend to myself and others.

I create meaningful and lasting friendships.

I cherish my friendships.

I am surrounded by friends who love and

support me.

Notes

_____

_____

_____

_____

_____

_____

_____

_____

_____

_____

_____

_____

_____

_____

_____

magic
moments

friendship

Family Relationships

I am loved and supported by my family.

I am a source of love and strength for my family.

I nurture positive and healthy family relationships.

I am grateful for my family's love and support.

I bring joy and positivity to my family.

I am a loving and caring family member.

I appreciate my family's unique qualities.

I communicate openly and honestly with my family.

I create harmonious and loving family relationships.

I am a pillar of strength for my family.

I am grateful for the lessons my family has taught

me.

I honor and respect my family's traditions.

I contribute to a loving and supportive family

environment.

I am a source of positivity and encouragement for

my family.

I am patient and understanding with my family.

I am grateful for the unconditional love of my family.

I cherish the moments I share with my family.

I am a loving and supportive family member.

I am proud of my family's accomplishments.

I am blessed to have a loving and supportive family.

Notes

THANKFUL
grateful
BLESSED
memories

Self-Expression

I express myself confidently and freely.

My voice deserves to be heard.

I am creative and full of unique ideas.

I am proud of my self-expression.

I communicate my thoughts and feelings with

ease.

I am confident in my self-expression.

I embrace my creativity.

I am not afraid to express my true self.

I am a unique and valuable individual.

I am proud of my artistic expression.

I share my thoughts and ideas with confidence.

I am a creative and expressive individual.

I am confident in my ability to communicate.

I express myself authentically.

I am proud of my unique voice.

I am a powerful and effective communicator.

I am fearless in expressing my true self.

I celebrate my creativity and self-expression.

I am a confident and expressive individual.

I am proud of my self-expression.

Notes

Mental Health

I prioritize my mental well-being.

I am worthy of self-care and love.

I am strong enough to ask for help when I

need it.

I am patient and kind to myself.

I am in control of my mental health.

I deserve to feel happy and healthy.

I am resilient in my mental health journey.

I am capable of overcoming any mental health

challenges.

I am proud of my mental health progress.

I am committed to my mental well-being.

I take care of my mind, body, and spirit.

I am deserving of mental health support.

I am not defined by my mental health struggles.

I am proud of my mental health journey.

I am worthy of inner peace and happiness.

I am capable of maintaining my mental health.

I am a priority in my own life.

I am kind and compassionate to myself.

I am strong and resilient in my mental health journey.

I am worthy of mental well-being and happiness.

Notes

_____

_____

_____

_____

_____

_____

_____

_____

_____

_____

_____

_____

_____

_____

_____

_____

I AM Enough

HEALTHY MIND

HAPPY HEART

Self-Respect

I respect myself and my boundaries.

I deserve to be treated with respect.

I honor my needs and desires.

I am worthy of respect and love.

I am proud of who I am.

I respect myself enough to walk away from

negativity.

I am deserving of self-respect.

I am confident in my self-worth.

I treat myself with kindness and respect.

I honor my values and beliefs.

I am proud of my integrity.

I am worthy of respect from others.

I demand respect in all areas of my life.

I am proud of my self-respect.

I respect my time and energy.

I treat myself with dignity and grace.

I am confident in my self-respect.

I honor and respect my body, mind, and soul.

I am a person of great worth and value.

I respect my journey and growth.

Notes

Body Positivity

I love and appreciate my body.

My body is strong and capable.

I am comfortable in my own skin.

I honor my body by treating it with kindness.

I embrace my natural beauty.

My body is a temple, and I respect it.

I am proud of my unique features.

I celebrate my body and all it does for me.

I love and accept my body as it is.

My body deserves love and respect.

I am beautiful just the way I am.

I am grateful for my healthy body.

I embrace my body's uniqueness.

I am kind and gentle with my body.

I am proud of my body's strength and

resilience.

I love every part of my body.

My body is beautiful and unique.

I nourish my body with love and care.

I am proud of my body's ability to heal and

thrive.

I love my body for all it allows me to do.

Notes

love
YOUR
body

all
bodies
ARE
good
bodies

Dear Body,
I love you

Empowerment

I am a powerful and influential individual.

I have the power to change the world.

I am capable of achieving great things.

I am a leader in my own life.

I am confident in my abilities.

I am in control of my destiny.

I am empowered to create positive change.

I am a force for good in the world.

I am proud of my accomplishments.

I am confident in my ability to make a

difference.

I am an empowered and confident individual.

I am a source of inspiration to others.

I am strong, capable, and empowered.

I am fearless and determined.

I am in charge of my own happiness.

I am empowered to pursue my dreams.

I am confident in my ability to succeed.

I am proud of my strength and resilience.

I am an empowered and courageous individual.

I am unstoppable when I believe in myself.

Notes

Stronger
THAN
Yesterday

Dreams and Goals

I am capable of achieving my dreams.

I am dedicated to reaching my goals.

I am confident in my ability to succeed.

I believe in the power of my dreams.

I am worthy of achieving my goals.

I am determined to make my dreams a reality.

I am focused on my goals and aspirations.

I am capable of overcoming any obstacle in

my path.

I am committed to my dreams and goals.

I am confident in my ability to achieve greatness

I am proud of my progress and achievements.

I am motivated to pursue my dreams.

I am deserving of all the success I achieve.

I am confident in my ability to make my
dreams come true.

I am capable of achieving anything I set my
mind to.

I am dedicated to my goals and aspirations.

I am confident in my ability to reach my
dreams.

I am worthy of achieving my highest potential.

I am motivated and determined to succeed.

I am proud of my dreams and goals.

Notes

I am confident in my ability to make my

dreams come true.

I am capable of achieving anything I set my

mind to.

I am dedicated to my goals and aspirations.

I am confident in my ability to reach my

dreams.

I am worthy of achieving my highest potential.

Creativity

I am a creative and talented individual.

I embrace my creativity and imagination.

I am confident in my creative abilities.

I am proud of my artistic expression.

I am a source of creative inspiration.

I am open to new and creative ideas.

I am confident in my ability to create.

I am proud of my creative talents.

I am a creative problem-solver.

I embrace my unique creative vision.

I am confident in my artistic abilities.

I am proud of my creative achievements.

I am a creative and innovative thinker.

I am inspired by the world around me.

I am confident in my ability to bring my

creative ideas to life.

I am proud of my creative journey.

I am a source of creative energy.

I embrace my creative passions.

I am confident in my ability to create beauty.

I am proud of my creative expression.

Notes

HAPPINESS
is not
out there,
it's in
You

Gratitude

I am grateful for all the blessings in my life.

I appreciate the little things that bring me joy.

I am thankful for my family and friends.

I am grateful for my health and well-being.

I am thankful for the love and support I receive.

I am grateful for the opportunities in my life.

I appreciate the beauty around me.

I am thankful for my growth and progress.

I am grateful for the lessons I have learned.

I appreciate the abundance in my life.

I am thankful for my unique talents and abilities.

I am grateful for the love and kindness in my life.

I appreciate the journey I am on.

I am thankful for the experiences that shape me.

I am grateful for the positive energy in my life.

I appreciate the support and encouragement

I receive.

I am thankful for my inner strength.

I am grateful for the love I give and receive.

I appreciate the joy and happiness in my life.

I am thankful for the gift of today.

Notes

Self-Improvement

I am committed to my personal growth.

I am always striving to be the best version of myself.

I am dedicated to my self-improvement journey.

I am proud of my progress and achievements.

I am open to learning and growing.

I am committed to becoming a better person every day.

I am confident in my ability to improve myself.

I am proud of my dedication to self-improvement.

I am constantly evolving and growing.

I am committed to becoming the best version of myself.

I am proud of my self-improvement journey.

I am dedicated to my personal development.

I am open to new experiences and
opportunities for growth.

I am committed to learning and growing
every day.

I am proud of my progress and
accomplishments.

I am confident in my ability to improve
and grow.

I am dedicated to becoming a better person.

I am committed to my self-improvement goals.

I am proud of my dedication to
personal growth.

I am constantly striving to better myself.

Notes

_____

_____

_____

_____

_____

_____

_____

_____

_____

_____

_____

_____

_____

_____

_____

_____

_____

_____

_____

_____

trust THE process

BELIEVE

GROW LOVE

Leadership

I am a natural-born leader.

I am confident in my ability to lead.

I inspire others with my leadership.

I am a positive and influential leader.

I am proud of my leadership abilities.

I am confident in my ability to guide others.

I am a strong and effective leader.

I am a source of inspiration and motivation.

I am confident in my leadership skills.

I am proud of my leadership achievements.

I am a compassionate and understanding leader.

I am confident in my ability to make a difference.

I am a powerful and influential leader.

I am proud of my leadership journey.

I am a positive role model for others.

I am confident in my ability to lead by example.

I am a strong and confident leader.

I am proud of my ability to inspire and guide others.

I am a capable and effective leader.

I am confident in my ability to create positive change.

Notes

YES YOU CAN !!!

Positive Mindset

I am a positive and optimistic individual.

I focus on the good in every situation.

I choose to see the best in myself and others.

I am grateful for all the positive experiences

in my life.

I embrace positivity and joy.

I am confident in my ability to maintain a

positive mindset.

I am proud of my positive outlook on life.

I am a source of positivity and light.

I am committed to maintaining a positive

attitude.

I am confident in my ability to stay positive.

I am proud of my positive mindset.

I embrace positivity and happiness.

I am grateful for the positive energy in my life.

I am a beacon of positivity and hope.

I am committed to maintaining a positive

outlook.

I am proud of my ability to stay positive.

I am confident in my ability to find the good in

every situation.

I choose to focus on the positive aspects of

life.

I am a positive and uplifting individual.

Notes

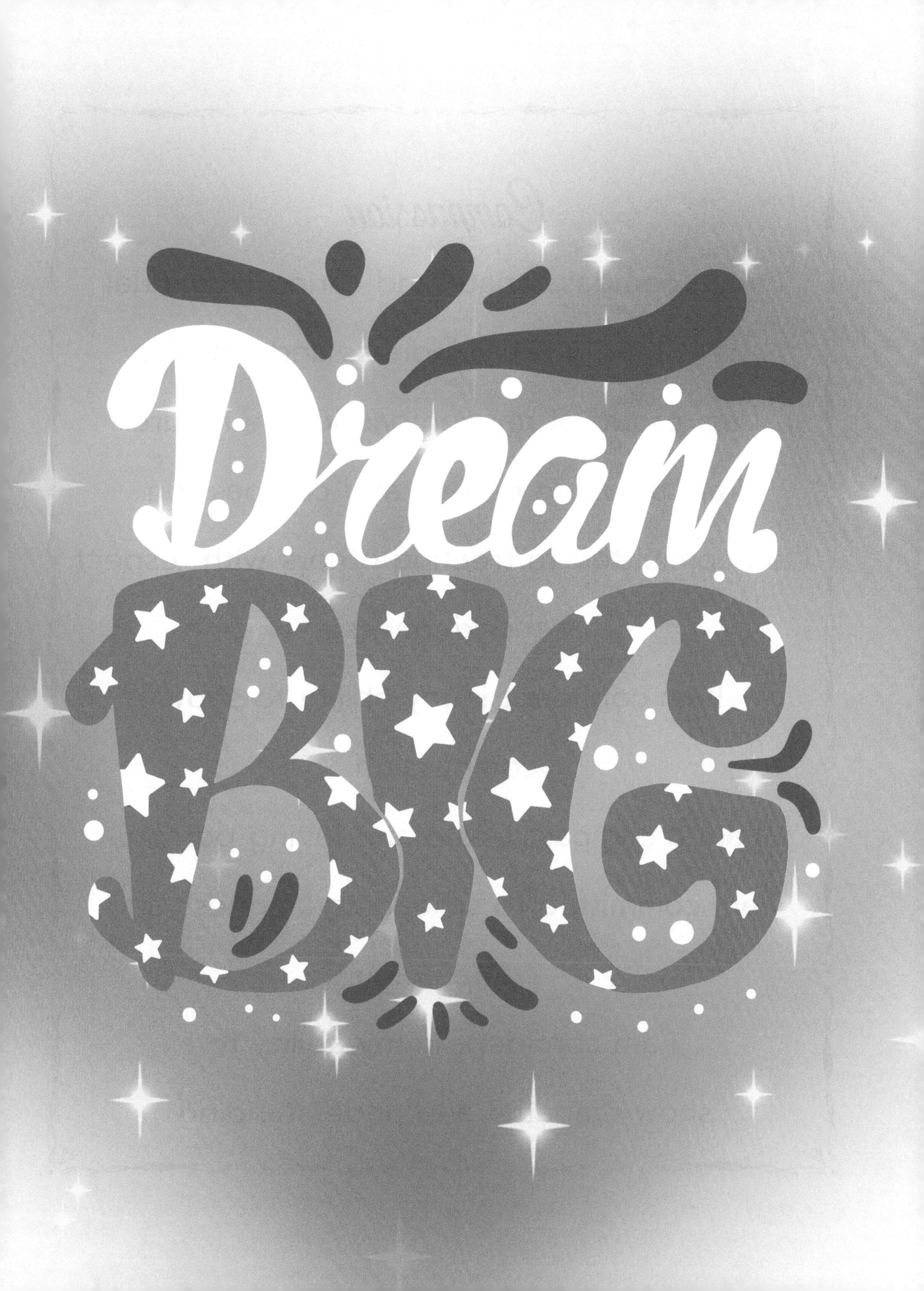
Dream
BIG

Compassion

I am a compassionate and caring individual.

I treat others with kindness and empathy.

I am proud of my compassionate nature.

I am a source of love and compassion.

I am committed to treating others with respect and kindness.

I am confident in my ability to show compassion.

I am a compassionate and loving person.

I am committed to spreading kindness and compassion.

I am confident in my ability to show empathy and understanding.

I treat myself and others with compassion.

I am proud of my ability to uplift and support others.

I am a source of comfort and kindness.

I am dedicated to showing compassion in all my actions.

I embrace my compassionate and caring nature.

I treat everyone with love and respect.

I am proud of my compassionate heart.

I choose to be a beacon of kindness and compassion.

I am grateful for my ability to understand and empathize with others.

Notes

CREATE YOUR destiny

SPREAD KINDNESS

embrace imperfection

STAY TRUE BE KIND

Empowering Others

I have the power to inspire and uplift others.

I encourage and support those around me.

I am a source of strength and inspiration

for others.

I use my voice to empower and motivate others.

I am proud of my ability to encourage and

uplift others.

I lead by example and inspire others to be their

best selves.

I am a positive influence on those around me.

I am committed to empowering others through

my actions and words.

I believe in the potential and greatness of others.

I am proud of my ability to inspire and empower those around me.

I support and uplift others in their journey.

I am a catalyst for positive change in the lives of others.

I encourage others to believe in themselves.

I am a source of hope and empowerment for others.

I use my experiences to empower and guide others.

I am dedicated to helping others reach their full potential.

Notes

Made in the USA
Monee, IL
13 December 2024

73530048R00050